# THE MISSISSIPPI

Maison de Ville, New Orleans

COUNTRY INNS OF AMERICA

# The
# Mississippi

A GUIDE TO THE INNS OF
LOUISIANA, MISSISSIPPI, ALABAMA, TENNESSEE,
ARKANSAS, MISSOURI, AND KENTUCKY

WRITTEN AND PHOTOGRAPHED BY
CHUCK LAWLISS

DESIGNED BY ROBERT REID

HOLT, RINEHART AND WINSTON, *New York*

AN OWL BOOK

*Front Cover:* Oak Alley, a classic Mississippi river plantation at Vacherie, Louisiana.

*Frontispiece:* The Beaumont Inn, Harrodsburg, Kentucky, pays homage to the great Confederate leader, General Robert E. Lee.

*Back Cover:* Barn at Shaker Village, Harrodsburg, Kentucky.

Maps by Anthony St. Aubyn.
Editorial Assistance by Margaret Kaufman.

Photographs on the following pages are used with permission from The Knapp Press, 5900 Wilshire Blvd., LA 90036, © 1978 by Knapp Communications Corporation: 1, 14, 15, 16, 17.

Published by Holt, Rinehart and Winston, 383 Madison Avenue, New York, New York 10017.
Published simultaneously in Canada by
Holt, Rinehart and Winston of Canada, Limited.

Library of Congress Cataloging in Publication Data

Lawliss, Chuck.
  The Mississippi.

  (Country inns of America)
  "An Owl book."
  1. Hotels, taverns, etc.—Mississippi River Region—Directories.  I. Title.  II. Series.
TX907.L38  1983    647′.97601    82-21171
ISBN 0-03-062212-3

First Edition

10 9 8 7 6 5 4 3 2 1

*A Robert Reid — Wieser & Wieser Production*

Printed in the United States of America

ISBN 0-03-062212-3

# THE INNS

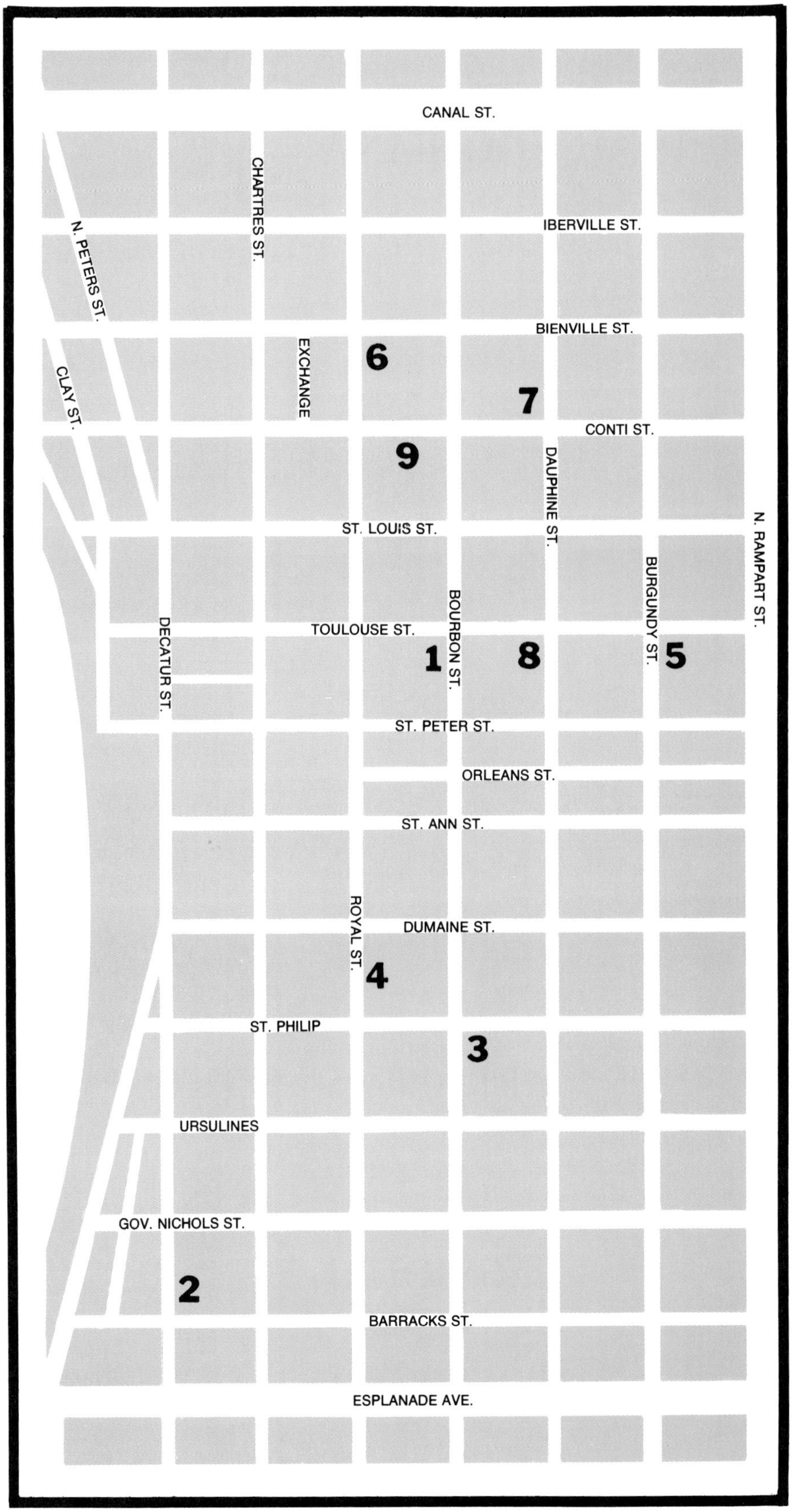

CANAL ST.
IBERVILLE ST.
BIENVILLE ST.
CONTI ST.
ST. LOUIS ST.
TOULOUSE ST.
ST. PETER ST.
ORLEANS ST.
ST. ANN ST.
DUMAINE ST.
ST. PHILIP
URSULINES
GOV. NICHOLS ST.
BARRACKS ST.
ESPLANADE AVE.
N. PETERS ST.
CLAY ST.
CHARTRES ST.
EXCHANGE
DECATUR ST.
ROYAL ST.
BOURBON ST.
DAUPHINE ST.
BURGUNDY ST.
N. RAMPART ST.
6
7
9
1
8
5
4
3
2

## New Orleans

MAISON DE VILLE 1
LE RICHELIEU 2
LAFITTE GUEST HOUSE 3
CORNSTALK GUEST HOUSE 4
MAISON DUPUY 5
THE ST. LOUIS 6
PRINCE CONTI 7
HOTEL MARIE ANTOINETTE 8
THE SAINT ANN 9
THE COLUMNS
PARK VIEW GUEST HOUSE
PONTCHARTRAIN
THE MISSISSIPPI QUEEN

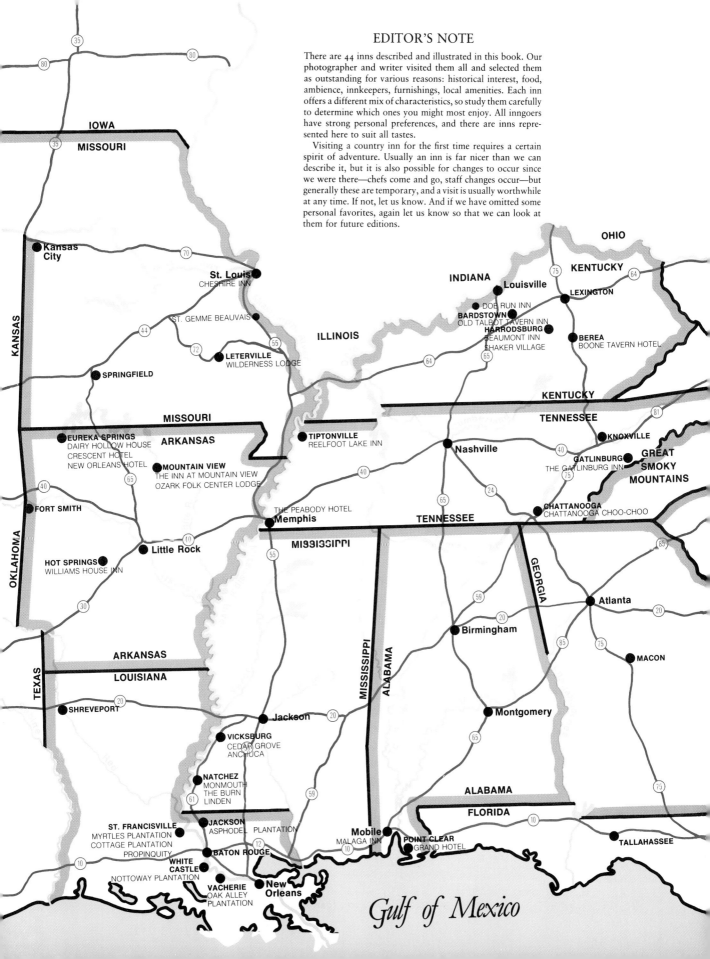

## EDITOR'S NOTE

There are 44 inns described and illustrated in this book. Our photographer and writer visited them all and selected them as outstanding for various reasons: historical interest, food, ambience, innkeepers, furnishings, local amenities. Each inn offers a different mix of characteristics, so study them carefully to determine which ones you might most enjoy. All inngoers have strong personal preferences, and there are inns represented here to suit all tastes.

Visiting a country inn for the first time requires a certain spirit of adventure. Usually an inn is far nicer than we can describe it, but it is also possible for changes to occur since we were there—chefs come and go, staff changes occur—but generally these are temporary, and a visit is usually worthwhile at any time. If not, let us know. And if we have omitted some personal favorites, again let us know so that we can look at them for future editions.

IOWA
MISSOURI

Kansas City

St. Louis
CHESHIRE INN

ST. GEMME BEAUVAIS

LETERVILLE
WILDERNESS LODGE

SPRINGFIELD

MISSOURI
ARKANSAS

EUREKA SPRINGS
DAIRY HOLLOW HOUSE
CRESCENT HOTEL
NEW ORLEANS HOTEL

MOUNTAIN VIEW
THE INN AT MOUNTAIN VIEW
OZARK FOLK CENTER LODGE

FORT SMITH

HOT SPRINGS
WILLIAMS HOUSE INN

Little Rock

OKLAHOMA

ARKANSAS

LOUISIANA

TEXAS

SHREVEPORT

THE PEABODY HOTEL
Memphis

MISSISSIPPI

ILLINOIS

TIPTONVILLE
REELFOOT LAKE INN

Nashville

TENNESSEE

Jackson

VICKSBURG
CEDAR GROVE
ANCHUCA

NATCHEZ
MONMOUTH
THE BURN
LINDEN

ST. FRANCISVILLE
MYRTLES PLANTATION
COTTAGE PLANTATION
PROPINQUITY

WHITE CASTLE
NOTTOWAY PLANTATION

JACKSON
ASPHODEL PLANTATION

BATON ROUGE

VACHERIE
OAK ALLEY PLANTATION

New Orleans

MISSISSIPPI

ALABAMA

Birmingham

Montgomery

ALABAMA

FLORIDA

Mobile
MALAGA INN

POINT CLEAR
GRAND HOTEL

OHIO

KENTUCKY

INDIANA

Louisville

LEXINGTON

DOE RUN INN
BARDSTOWN
OLD TALBOT TAVERN INN
HARRODSBURG
BEAUMONT INN
SHAKER VILLAGE

BEREA
BOONE TAVERN HOTEL

KENTUCKY

TENNESSEE

KNOXVILLE

GATLINBURG
THE GATLINBURG INN

GREAT SMOKY MOUNTAINS

CHATTANOOGA
CHATTANOOGA CHOO-CHOO

GEORGIA

Atlanta

MACON

TALLAHASSEE

Gulf of Mexico

# Last but not least

This impressive four-story classic building was built in 1974 of two-hundred-year-old brick and replaced seven nondescript structures, including a blacksmith shop and a Chinese laundry. It was the last hotel the historic commission permitted to be built in the French Quarter and it ended two decades of growth on a high note. Under the watchful eye of Austrian innkeeper Eric Winkler it has achieved parity with its illustrious neighbors. Travel columnist Horace Sutton named this "highly polished, trim little inn" one of his ten favorite hotels in America. It also is a favorite of a number of show business celebrities, including Elizabeth Taylor and Johnny Carson.

The guest rooms and public areas are furnished in French country provincial. The dining room is Le Bon Creole, offering both Cajun and Creole specialties: crayfish Creole, catfish Manchac, Louisiana quail

*Left.* Le Bon Creole, the setting for delectable dining.

and crabmeat etouffée. The Cabaret Lautrec is delightfully decorated with life-sized murals à la the diminutive master.

MAISON DUPUY, 101 Toulouse Street, New Orleans, LA 70112; (504)586-8000 (toll free from out of state, 1-800 535-9177); Eric V. Winkler, General Manager. A new 226-room hotel on the edge of the French Quarter with all the charm of Old New Orleans. Open all year. Rates range from $90 to $130, single occupancy; $100 to $140, double occupancy, with suites to $800. The 120-seat restaurant, Le Bon Creole, is open to the public 3 meals a day and offers Creole and Cajun specialities. There is entertainment in the colorful Toulouse Lautrec lounge from 5 to 1 A.M. Children welcome. No pets. American Express, Diners Club, Carte Blanche, MasterCard and Visa credit cards are accepted. There is a swimming pool in the courtyard, a gift shop, and free shoe shines.

DIRECTIONS: See map in front of book.

# New Orleans CORNSTALK GUEST HOUSE LOUISIANA

## You've seen it in the movies

The Cornstalk is one of the most distinctive buildings in the French Quarter, a white Victorian mansion tucked in among the many stuccoed buildings with the more traditional forms of fancy iron grillwork. Its most memorable feature is its iron fence, shaped and painted to resemble tall corn. It was commissioned, they say, by the first owner, who wanted to ease the homesick heart of his young bride who missed her native Iowa.

The Cornstalk has been an inn since the middle 1940s and is now run by the granddaughter of the original innkeeper. She is planning an outdoor cafe for the garden in front of the house. The Cornstalk has also become quite a movie star, appearing in

*Mandingo,* two Charles Bronson films, *The Family* and *Hard Times,* and in Paul Newman's *The Drowning Pool.*

All the comfortable rooms are furnished with antiques, have fireplaces and private baths, and are centrally air conditioned.

To wake up at the Cornstalk with the sound of birds singing and the toot of steamboats on the river is to be transported back a century.

---

CORNSTALK GUEST HOUSE, 915 Royal Street, New Orleans, LA 70116; (504) 523-1515; David and Debbie Spencer, Innkeepers. This 16-room inn and its memorable iron fence is one of the landmarks in the French Quarter. Open all year. Rates for double occupancy, $60 to $85. A Continental breakfast is included. An outdoor French cafe will be opened in 1983. Children welcome. No pets. American Express, MasterCard and Visa credit cards accepted. The Cornstalk is ideally located for easy access to the attractions of the French Quarter.

DIRECTIONS: See map in front of book.

*Left.* The house is named after the magnificent iron fence, built to resemble an Iowa corn field.

Each guest room is sumptuously furnished.

# THE SAINT LOUIS PRINCE CONTI

New Orleans

**LOUISIANA**

## A chain of French jewels

A brewery, a coffee factory, a private house, and a two-story lumberyard that had once been a market have all been magically transformed into jewel-like inns. The wand was in the hand of Mark C. Smith III, a New Orleans businessman now head of Century Management, the company which operates the inns. Each inn has as distinct a personality as the famous person for whom it was named; all are alike in their adherence to high standards of quality, superb taste, and attentive service.

If one can be singled out as the showcase it is THE SAINT LOUIS, once the Regal Brewery. It is named after Louis IX, who achieved sainthood by leading the Seventh Crusade. The Vieux Carré Commission chose it for its 1972 Award of Excellence. The hotel,

its exterior walls the color of a ripe cantaloupe, wraps around a fountained courtyard. The sixty-seven guest rooms are decorated with excellent Louis XV and XVI reproductions. Most of the bathrooms are equipped with bidets, and terrycloth bathrobes are provided for the guests.

A contemporary note is struck in the inn's new restaurant, L'Escale, where a brilliant use of pastels form a backdrop for the presentation of classic French cuisine. L'Escale is shamelessly expensive but one must remember that the chef, Jean-Louis Montestruck, is one of only two *maitre cuisiniers de France* at work in this country.

The lobby of THE PRINCE CONTI, once a coffee factory, is appointed in the fashion of a French chateau with a stunning Baccarat chandelier and a Trumeau painting of the prince over a Louis XV marble mantle. The bedrooms are furnished with

A Prince Conti guest room.

An original Chippendale chest in the Saint Louis lobby.

# HOTEL MARIE ANTOINETTE
# THE SAINT ANN

Breakfast room of the Saint Ann.

antiques—one bedstead has a carved headboard displaying a bevy of naked Reubenesque beauties. There is no dining room but guests are served a complimentary Continental breakfast.

A first-class French restaurant, the Louis XVI, is to be found in the HOTEL MARIE ANTOINETTE. Among its offerings are an excellent paté, Russian caviar, boeuf Wellington perigourdine, and duckling roti au poivre vert. This former market and lumberyard is authentically decorated in period furnishings; both the Louis XVI and the small cocktail lounge are notable in their appointments.

THE SAINT ANN, formerly a private house, has a dining room open for breakfast and brunch only. It offers a mixture of Creole and Continental dishes, including particularly fine omelets. Many of the sixty guest rooms also are decorated with antiques.

---

THE SAINT LOUIS, 730 Bienville Street, New Orleans, LA 70130; (504) 581-7300 (toll free outside of state, 1-800 535-9741); Bret Smith, General Manager. Sixty-seven luxury guest rooms. Rates: $95 to $130, single occupancy; $105 to $140, double occupancy; suites $175 and up. Rates include Continental breakfast. L'Escale Restaurant offers classic French cuisine. American Express, Diners Club, Carte Blanche, MasterCard and Visa credit cards accepted. Children welcome ($12 charge). No pets.

PRINCE CONTI, 830 Rue Conti, New Orleans, LA 70140; (504) 529-4172 (toll free outside of state, 1-800 535-7908); Janet Robichaux, General Manager. A charming small hotel offering 50 rooms, mostly furnished with antiques. Rates: $60 to $125, single occupancy; $70 to $130, double occupancy; suites $150 to $275. Continental breakfast included in rates. American Express, Diners Club, Carte Blanche, MasterCard and Visa credit cards accepted. Children welcome. No pets.

HOTEL MARIE ANTOINETTE, 827 Toulouse Street, New Orleans, LA 70112; (504) 525-2300; Michael Howland, General Manager. Attractive French Quarter hotel with 93 rooms. Rates: $70 to $115, single occupancy; $80 to $125, double occupancy; suites $250 to $350. Dining room is Louis XVI Restaurant with excellent continental menu. American Express, Diners Club, Carte Blanche, MasterCard and Visa credit cards accepted. Children welcome. No pets. Swimming pool in courtyard.

THE SAINT ANN, 717 Conti Street, New Orleans, LA 70130; (504) 581-1881 (toll free outside of state, 1-800 535-9730); Jane Roberts, General Manager. Sixty-room French Quarter hotel with attractive courtyard. Rates: $65 to $110, single occupancy; $75 to $125, double occupancy; suites from $200. Hotel cafe open for breakfast and lunch with Creole and Continental menu. American Express, Diners Club, Carte Blanche, MasterCard and Visa credit cards accepted. Children welcome. No pets. Swimming pool in courtyard.

DIRECTIONS: All four hotels may be found on map in front of book.

# MAISON DE VILLE

New Orleans | LOUISIANA

## Perhaps the best small hotel in the country

Great things have been created here. Two centuries ago, the owner of this 1742 townhouse, a pharmacist named A. Peychaud, mixed a new drink containing bourbon and bitters, stirred it with the quill of a cock and *voila!*—the Sazerac, or "cocktail", was born. In the hotel's Audubon Cottages, a block away, the artist painted most of the Louisiana species for his famous *Birds of America.* More recently, Tennessee Williams polished his play, *A Streetcar Named Desire,* in the courtyard. Another notable achievement was that of owners Cornelius White and Terence Hall and manager William Prentiss, who took over the Maison de Ville when it was teetering on the edge of bankruptcy and turned it into what many consider to be the best small hotel in the country.

The Maison de Ville offers its guests three quite different types of accommodation. The high-ceilinged rooms in the main house are furnished with antiques, majestic four poster beds, marble basins, period paintings, and old brass fittings. In the rear of the courtyard are the slave quarters. There the rooms are less formal but equally comfortable. Wood ceilings painted white, brick walls, and fireplaces help set a mood of casual elegance. The Audubon Cottages are a cluster of six small houses behind a high stucco wall. Some are among the oldest structures in the French Quarter, others are contemporary, but they blend together beautifully and harmoniously. Here the feeling is country: exposed beam-and-plank ceilings, brick walls, and slate or terra cotta tile floors. A swimming pool in the center of the court is the one discreet contemporary note. Most of the cottages have full kitchens, and the refrigerators are well stocked with soft drinks, lemons, and mixers. The bustle of the nearby French Quarter seems many miles away.

The service at the hotel would do the Ritz proud. A concierge handles dinner reservations and travel

The old slave quarters off the courtyard also house guests.

details with equal ease. Shoes left outside bedroom doors greet the dawn polished. And every morning each guest is brought a silver tray with freshly squeezed orange juice, croissants, a pot of coffee, and the *Times-Picayune.* On each tray is a single fresh rose. Beds are turned down at night, a small piece of foil-wrapped chocolate placed on the pillow.

The Maison de Ville is truly a haven, not only from the abrasions of a busy city but also from the cares of the modern world.

MAISON DE VILLE, 727 Toulouse Street, New Orleans, LA 70130; (504) 561-5858; William Prentiss, Innkeeper. An exquisite small hotel and cottage colony in the heart of the French Quarter. Open all year. Twenty-one rooms and 7 cottages, 5 with kitchens. Rates: from $90, single occupancy; from $100, double occupancy; suites from $185; cottages from $250. Rates include Continental breakfast, newspapers, afternoon tea or coffee, soft drinks and ice. No credit cards accepted. Children welcome. No pets. Swimming pool at the cottages.
DIRECTIONS: See map in front of book.

*Left.* The semitropical courtyard with its cast-iron fountain. OVERLEAF. A corner of the salon, left, and at right, the interior of one of the Audubon cottages.

ALL PHOTOGRAPHS OF MAISON DE VILLE BY GEORGE W. GARDNER

# LAFITTE GUEST HOUSE

New Orleans         **LOUISIANA**

## Memories of a pirate amid comforts of the past

Reminders of the flamboyant French pirate Jean Lafitte abound in the French Quarter. One of the oldest buildings there is the Lafitte Blacksmith Shop, which he is reported to have used as an office. Across the street is the Lafitte Guest House, an 1849 typically Vieux Carré three-story structure that has been restored by Steve Guyton and his parents and furnished with period antiques. The fourteen guest rooms are spacious and comfortable, many with crystal chandeliers and fireplaces with their original black marble mantels. Five rooms with sleeping lofts and exposed brick walls are in the adjacent slave quarters. A breakfast of freshly squeezed juice, croissants with jam and butter, and coffee or tea brightens the morning.

LAFITTE GUEST HOUSE, 1003 Bourbon Street, New Orleans, LA 70116; (504) 581-2678 (toll free from outside of state, 1-800 223-6625); Steve Guyton, Innkeeper. An 1849 private residence restored and converted to a delightful inn with 14 guest rooms furnished with antiques. Open all year. Rates range from $48 to $70 single occupancy; $58 to $80 double occupancy, with a $10 charge for each additional person. A Continental breakfast is included in the rates. Children welcome. No pets. American Express, MasterCard and Visa credit cards are accepted.

DIRECTIONS: See map in front of book.

A guest suite, showing exposed brick common throughout the inn.

## A medley of macaroni factory and Greek Revival

When former Beatle Paul McCartney and his family were in New Orleans a few years ago, they holed up in a suite at Le Richelieu. An excellent choice: the hotel protected their privacy and saw to their comfort. Le Richelieu gets good press. The New Orleans *Times-Picayune* called it "the ultimate in in-town living." *Business Week* said it has "The South's most luxurious suite." The hotel was created from two adjacent old French Quarter buildings: an 1850 Greek Revival house (one of five in a row built by a father for his children), and a 1902 four-story macaroni factory. The result is more than pleasing. The hotel has a garden courtyard with a small swimming pool, and a bar that is frequented by New Orleanians who live near the hotel. Joanne Kirkpatrick manages the inn with competence and good humor. (Note: don't let the term "motor hotel" mislead you. In the French Quarter it simply means that there is parking, which is very hard to come by there.)

LE RICHELIEU MOTOR HOTEL, 1234 Chartres Street, New Orleans, LA 70116; (504) 529-2492 (toll free outside of state, 1-800 535-8653); Frank S. Rochefort, Jr., Owner. A handsome 88-room inn in the quiet part of the French Quarter. Open all year. Rates by room range from $55 to $80; the 17 suites, from $85 to $300. The Terrace Cafe is open to the public from 7:30 A.M. to 8:45 P.M., serving light Continental fare. Children are welcome ($10 per child charge). No pets; New Orleans law prohibits pets in hotels. American Express, Diners Club, Carte Blanche, MasterCard and Visa credit cards accepted. There is a swimming pool in the courtyard, and the hotel is an easy walk from the attractions of the French Quarter.

DIRECTIONS: See map in front of book.

The courtyard and swimming pool viewed from a guest room.

# New Orleans PONTCHARTRAIN HOTEL LOUISIANA

## A family affair to remember

In an age when hotels run to cookie-cutter similarity and the term "hotel food" is considered pejorative, the Pontchartrain is a serendipitous choice of lodgings in the Crescent City. The rooms are spacious, luxuriously appointed, and furnished with a flair that would give a hotel-chain cost accountant cardiac arrest. The hotel's restaurant, the Caribbean Room, is the peer of any in this city where four stars are as common as at a meeting of the Joint Chiefs of Staff. It should come as no surprise to the knowledgable that the Pontchartrain is family-run. And what an amazing family it is.

The hotel, owned and managed by Albert L. Aschaffenburg, "Mr. Albert" to the staff, was started by his grandfather, a New Orleans hotelier, who dreamed of building a luxury apartment hotel. The grandfather died before he could build the Pontchartrain, but his son made the dream come true, and the new hotel opened on St. Charles Avenue in 1927. Eighteen fortunate permanent residents are happily ensconced in the hotel, and in the 1960s a wealthy New Orleanian spent a small fortune building a penthouse apartment here, his decision a tribute to the quality of the Pontchartrain.

Mention the Pontchartrain to a member of the southern aristocracy and you usually will be told of some personal kindness performed by the Aschaffenburg family. Meet Mr. Aschaffenburg and you will understand: he is southern charm personified and his concern for his guests and his attention to detail is prodigious. He takes great pride, for example, in remembering the birthdays and anniversaries of his regular patrons.

The warm, softly lighted Caribbean Room is the crown jewel of the hotel. The basic menu was worked out by Mr. Aschaffenburg's father and Nathaniel

Third generation hotelman Albert Aschaffenburg, the innkeeper *par excellence*.

Burton, a Mississippi black who was a completely self-taught cook. Fresh Gulf fish and sea food are prepared with a regional flair. Specialities include soft shell crabs amandine, backfin lump crabmeat au gratin, pompano Pontchartrain (pompano broiled in butter and topped with a succulent Buster Crab), and a dessert that is fondly remembered by tens of thousands of former guests: the Pontchartrain's famous Mile High Ice Cream Pie.

PONTCHARTRAIN HOTEL, 2031 St. Charles Avenue, New Orleans, LA 70140; (504) 524-0581; Albert Aschaffenburg, President. Luxurious and charming 100-room hotel catering to the carriage trade. Open all year. Rates range from $75 to $105, single occupancy; $85 to $125, double occupancy; suites to $325. Public dining room in famed Caribbean Room, serving Creole and Cajun specialities. Children welcome. No pets. American Express, Diners Club, MasterCard and Visa credit cards accepted.

DIRECTIONS: Royal becomes St. Charles after Canal Street.

*Left.* A rather nice four-room suite—the one used by Philippe Entremont, conductor of the New Orleans Symphony, when he is in town.

# New Orleans PARK VIEW GUEST HOUSE LOUISIANA

## A newly restored period house

The doldrums that engulfed New Orleans after the Civil War ended with the excitement that accompanied the Cotton Exposition of 1884, held in the great park out on St. Charles Avenue. This stone Victorian was built as a guest house on the far edge of the park in anticipation of the influx of well-heeled visitors. It continued as a boarding house for many years, fell into disrepair, and in 1978 was bought by Zafir Zaitoon, a young Lebanese dentist, who has returned it to its glory days. It commands a beautiful view of what is now Audubon Park, and is a short walk from Tulane, Loyola, and the other colleges in the area.

The rooms are decorated in period furniture, and most have the massive beds which are unique to the area. Stained-glass windows provide a pleasant counterpoint to the sweeping vistas, and several of the upstairs rooms have private balconies facing the park.

PARK VIEW GUEST HOUSE, 7004 St. Charles Avenue, New Orleans, LA 70118; (504) 866-7564; Zafir B. Zaitoon, Innkeeper. There are 25 guest rooms in this Victorian guest house built for the Cotton Exhibition of 1884. Open all year. Rates range from $28 to $35, single occupancy; $38 to $55, double occupancy, all with shared baths, to $40 to $55, double occupancy with private bath. There is an additional $10 charge per person for more than two in a room. A Continental breakfast is included in the rates. Neither children nor pets are welcome. American Express, MasterCard and Visa credit cards are accepted. The inn is adjacent to the city's beautiful 400-acre Audubon Park.

DIRECTIONS: Royal becomes St. Charles after Canal Street.

# THE COLUMNS

New Orleans      **LOUISIANA**

## Perfect for watching the Mardi Gras parades

In 1883, architect Thomas Sully built this Italianate Victorian mansion in the area of the city known then as the American Section. Originally built for a rich Jewish merchant, the mansion became a boarding house in 1913, and in 1980 Jacques and Claire Creppel undertook a massive refurbishing and converted it into an inn. They succeeded splendidly; the Columns now offers a quiet haven in bustling New Orleans, where the shade trees and twelve-foot ceilings offer cool relief from the summer heat. Off the lobby is an inviting bar, and dining here is a pleasure in a city known for culinary pleasures.

For those who want to see the Mardi Gras without the frenzy of the French Quarter, the porch is perfect for viewing the justly famous parades. The Columns also is an excellent base for exploring the architectural wonders of the Garden District.

THE COLUMNS, 3811 St. Charles Street, New Orleans, LA 70114; (504) 899-9308; Jacques and Claire Creppel, Innkeepers. A restored Italianate Victorian mansion in the lovely Garden District of the city. Open all year. Rates for the 25 guest rooms range from $35 to $75 per room with a $5 charge for each person beyond two in the room. Dining room is open to the public for 3 meals a day and high tea. Children welcome. No pets. American Express, MasterCard and Visa credit cards accepted.

DIRECTIONS: Royal becomes St. Charles after Canal Street.

Innkeeper Jacques Creppel.

New Orleans     # MISSISSIPPI QUEEN     **LOUISIANA**

## "Steamboating is an incurable disease . . ."

Richard Bissell, *A Stretch on the River*

To cut to the heart of the matter, the *Mississippi Queen* is as handsome and luxurious as any cruise ship afloat today. She should be. She was designed by James Gardner of London, designer of Cunard's *QE II,* and cost twenty-seven million dollars. She offers her guests elevators, a swimming pool, sauna and gym, a beauty shop, a movie theatre, and total air conditioning with individual control in each cabin. Throughout the boat there is brass trim, zinc paneling, and brilliant mirrors. There are steel and brass dance floors and plush carpeting throughout the interior spaces. She is ultra modern and, at the same time, a full-fledged sister to every great steamship that ever

*Left.* The paddle wheeler docked at Vicksburg.

worked the river. The food, supervised by Lou Moses, is magnificent. Mr. Moses, a Dutchman born into the hotel and restaurant business, has thirty-five years of experience in Europe, on the Holland America Lines, and in hosteleries here. One savors such specialities as oysters Vieux Carré, stuffed Cornish hen, poached filet of red snapper, filet of sole Marguerey, and prime ribs of beef.

There is one special thing about sailing on the *Mississippi Queen* that no sea-going cruise ship can match. Once out of sight of land, every ocean looks the same. Ocean air is invigorating but the view is dull, dull, dull. Cruising the Mississippi, on the other hand, is fascinating and ever-changing. And the Queen puts in at delightful ports of call: stately antebellum plantation houses right by the levee, Natchez,

Lively Dixieland jazz is a nightly feature.

Vicksburg, and Memphis—there is plenty to do and see whatever portion of the 1,700-mile river one chooses to cruise.

Best of all, steamboating is an historic part of the American experience: Mark Twain, riverboat gamblers, "Show Boat," decks piled high with bales of cotton, "Waitin' for the Robert E. Lee," the authoritative toot of the whistle, the calliope serenade as the Queen leaves the dock—one would need a particularly thick skin to remain impervious to such nostalgia as this. At the stern is the Paddle Wheel Lounge where one can sit of an evening watching the paddle wheel churn. The traffic on the river is seen through a wall of glass while a honky-tonk piano and a banjo play New Orleans jazz and other river music. After a while, steaming on the river, one is struck by the realization that there is no place in the world one would rather be.

MISSISSIPPI QUEEN, 511 Main St., Cincinnati, Ohio 45202; —800) 543-1949; in Ohio (800) 582-1888; Tom Murphy Chief Purser. The new, luxurious 396-passenger sister boat to the *Delta Queen*. Operates all year. Rates range from $255 for a 3-night round-trip cruise from New Orleans to $3790 for a 14-day cruise from St. Paul to New Orleans, rates varying by type of accommodation. Rates include all meals. For a complete list of rates and the variety of cruises, consult your travel agent or write for handsome illustrated color brochure. Children welcome; no pets. American Express credit card accepted.

DIRECTIONS: In St. Louis, at foot of Gateway Arch; in New Orleans, at International Passenger Terminal.

*Right*. The grand staircase between decks.

The main dining room, where oysters and crayfish are specialities.

## An incomparable setting for a magnificent house

In the early 1700s, a now-forgotten French settler built a small house here and planted twenty-eight live oaks in two rows of fourteen, eighty feet apart. Over the centuries their branches have intertwined to form a glorious tunnel, an *allée*, from the Great River Road to the classic pink main house. Twenty-eight more live oaks are similarly placed at the rear of the house. The mansion itself was built in 1839 by Jacques Telesphore Roman, a sugar planter, for his young bride. Oak Alley survived the Civil War intact, but its owner did not fare so well. The estate was sold at auction in 1866 for $32,800. After a succession of owners it was abandoned, and was deteriorating badly when Andrew and Josephine Stewart bought it in 1925. They restored it—the first of the Great River Road plantations to be fully restored—lived in it for a number of years, and left it to a family foundation in 1972. Mrs. Stewart's great nephew, Zeb Mayhew, Jr., now manages the property with his wife, Lorraine.

The interior of Oak Alley is as Mrs. Stewart left it. The furniture, mainly antique, is arranged in the style of the 1920s. Mr. Stewart, a retired New Orleans cotton broker, had a bad heart and a lift was installed on the main staircase to take him up and down. The changes made at Oak Alley show the difference between French and American traditions: the French had the living room on the second floor, the Stewarts changed it to the first; the French had a circular stairway curving from what is now the living room to the second floor, the Stewarts put a straight stairway in the hallway.

In French times, the kitchen was in a separate building, to isolate its heat and odors. Food was brought to the table by a "whistling boy," so called because he was required to whistle along the way to prove that he wasn't sampling the dishes. On partic-

ularly hot days, a block of ice was placed on the dining room table. A large punkah, or shoo-fly, was hung from the ceiling above the table, kept in motion by a young slave pulling a silk rope. An 1854 ledger showed that 300 pounds of ice was delivered to Oak Alley each week during the hot months at a total cost for the summer of one hundred and fifty-four dollars. In those days, ice from New England lakes was a profitable commodity to be shipped to southern ports.

There are four guest rooms with full kitchens in two nearby cabins. There is also a modest restaurant serving such regional dishes as red beans and rice, gumbo, and pecan pie.

OAK ALLEY, Box 10, Vacherie, LA 70090; (504) 265-2151; Zeb and Lorraine Mayhew, Jr., Innkeepers. Classic Mississippi River plantation in stunning setting of 28 live oaks in two rows reaching from house to the river. Open all year except Thanksgiving, Christmas and New Year's Day. Four guest suites with kitchen facilities in two rustic cabins nearby. Rates are $50 for double occupancy; $5 for each additional person, including children. Restaurant open to the public serving lunch only. Personal checks accepted with credit card. Children welcome. No pets. Gift shop.

DIRECTIONS: From Baton Rouge I-10 east to Sunshine Bridge exit, Rte. 18 south 15 miles to Oak Alley.

*Left.* Peace and tranquility among the massive live oaks.

# White Castle NOTTOWAY PLANTATION LOUISIANA

## "Build me the finest house on the river."

Nottoway is the largest and most ornate ante-bellum mansion in the South. With some one hundred and twenty-five thousand paying visitors annually, it is second only to the Superdome as the biggest tourist attraction in the state. Famed New Orleans architect Henry Howard blended Greek Revival and Italianate in designing this private residence for John Hampden Randolph, a sugar planter from Nottoway County, Virginia. Randolph had asked Howard to build him the finest house on the river, and his request was granted. The two-storied building is enclosed by balconies and Corinthian columns hand carved out of cypress. Inside are sixty-six rooms, a total of fifty-

*Left.* Nottoway's spacious stairway leads to the plantation's 66 rooms.

three thousand square feet. The most unusual is the ballroom, the walls a soft yellow and the maple floors painted white. The large windows open out to permit couples to dance on the balcony. Eight of Mr. Randolph's children were girls, so the ballroom, presumably, was well used.

Undoubtedly, this was the most modern house in the South when it was completed in 1859. There are bathrooms with running water on each floor, the house was lit by gas, and there is an abundance of closets. (Under Spanish and French rule houses were taxed for each closet, which accounts for the popularity of armoires in this area.)

Nottoway was a private home until 1980, when it was purchased by Arlin Dease of Baton Rouge, a builder who had restored several plantation houses

A private house until 1980.

in the area. A condition of the sale was that the previous owner, Ms. Odessa Owen, would be given an apartment in the house for the rest of her life. Ms. Owen now enjoys mingling with the guests.

There are six guest rooms, all different, all lavishly furnished and opening onto the balcony or courtyard. The balcony overlooks the lovely oaks, a duck pond, and the Mississippi. Guests are greeted with a welcoming drink, and there are flowers in each room. A complimentary bottle of champagne is brought in the evening, and room service is available. A solid planter's breakfast—eggs benedict, freshly squeezed juice, and Creole coffee—fortifies one for the coming day. Lunch may be taken in the first-floor restaurant, and, on request, guests will be served dinner in the dining room for a surprisingly modest ten dollars (including wine). There is an attractive swimming pool, and a stroll through the gardens is a pleasure.

NOTTOWAY PLANTATION, Box 160, White Castle, LA 70788; (504) 545-2730; Arlin K. Dease, Innkeeper. Largest antebellum mansion in the South recently restored to its original grandeur. Open all year except Christmas. Six elegant guest rooms in mansion, all with period furnishings and private baths and opening onto the balcony or courtyard. Rates: $75, single occupancy; $105, double occupancy, and $132 for third person in room. Rates include plantation breakfast, tour, and champagne and fresh flowers in room on arrival. Dining room open to public at lunch. Dinner served in mansion dining room on request of guests; $10 per person charge including wine. MasterCard and Visa credit cards accepted. Swimming pool and lovely garden on grounds. Gift shop.

DIRECTIONS: From Baton Rouge, I-10 west to Plaquemine exit, Rte. 1 (Great River Road) south 18 miles to plantation.

The guest rooms are furnished according to old plantation records.

# MYRTLES PLANTATION

St. Francisville | LOUISIANA

## Love at first sight for two Californians

James and Frances Meyers had already restored a Victorian house in San Jose, California, when they took a vacation cruise on the *Mississippi Queen* and fell in love with the plantation country. Shortly thereafter they purchased the Myrtles. It was built in 1796 by General David Bradford, leader of the Pennsylvania Whiskey Rebellion of 1794, who had fled South to avoid capture. The entrance hall has stunning examples of *faux vois* and plaster friezes, and the handpainted and etched stained glass around the front door is original. Two parlors are mirror reflections of one another: twin marble mantles, chandeliers, French gilded mirrors, and identical friezes and medallions. On the outside of the house are two hundred and forty feet of ironwork.

There are six guest rooms in the main house, all furnished with antiques, and five in another building. A hearty breakfast of orange juice, bacon and eggs, grits, biscuits, and coffee is included.

THE MYRTLES PLANTATION, Box 387, St. Francisville, LA 70775; (504) 635-6277; James and Frances Meyers, Innkeepers. A restored 1796 French-style plantation, offering 11 guest accommodations. Open all year. Rates from $55 to $75, double occupancy. Rates include plantation breakfast. Dining room is open for groups touring the plantation. Children welcome ($10 charge for third person in room). No pets. MasterCard and Visa credit cards accepted. Guests may fish in stocked pond on grounds.

DIRECTIONS: One mile north of St. Francisville on US 61.

Charlotte McKeithen, one of the guides provided to show guests around.

# A friendly welcome in Audubon country

Propinquity is the home of Charles Seif, a retired Defense Department executive, and his wife Gladys, who had lived in this 1809 house as a child. The Seifs restored the house, the oldest in historic St. Francisville, furnished it with antiques, and now welcome guests to the two upstairs bedrooms, both equipped with private baths. They proudly give guests tours of the house and serve a complimentary breakfast that includes yellow grits, homemade fig preserves, and other southern specialities.

St. Francisville is Audubon country, and Propinquity boasts three originals: oil portraits of Juliana Randolph and her husband, James Alexander Stewart of Holly Grove Plantation, and an 1837 painting of a sharptailed grouse. The name Propinquity, explain the Seifs, "means close to history, kinfolk, friends, the street, the town, and the hearts of its owners."

PROPINQUITY, 523 Royal Street, St. Francisville, LA 70775; (504) 635-6855; Mr. and Mrs. Charles Seif, Innkeepers. A small, charming inn with 2 guest rooms in the heart of the Audubon country. Open all year. Rates for single or double occupancy, which includes Continental breakfast. Children welcome ($10 surcharge). No pets. No credit cards. The 4-acre grounds reward birdwatching.

DIRECTIONS: St. Francisville is 15 miles north of Baton Rouge off Rte. 61. The inn is in the town's historic district.

Audubon bird-watched here.

# St. Francisville COTTAGE PLANTATION LOUISIANA

## A television pioneer in a pioneer setting

Southern plantations tend to be Greek Revival or, in Louisiana, of French or Spanish influence. The Cottage is an exception, a raised English cottage of twenty rooms built in 1795. For many years the home of Thomas Butler, judge and later congressman, the Cottage today is beautifully preserved with most of the original furnishings. Of particular interest is the fact that all the original outbuildings are still intact: kitchen, milk house, the judge's office, carriage house, smokehouse, and three slave cabins. The one modern element is a swimming pool for the enjoyment of the guests.

The Cottage became an inn in 1951 and is owned by Robert and Martha Weller. Mr. Weller, a retired vice president of research and engineering at Zenith, was a pioneer in the development of television.

THE COTTAGE PLANTATION, Box 425, St. Francisville, LA 70775; (504) 635-3674; Robert and Martha Weller, Innkeepers. A restored English cottage of 20 rooms with all original outbuildings: milk house, kitchen, judge's office, carriage house, smokehouse, and 3 slave cabins. Open all year, except Christmas. Five guest rooms. Rates: $40, single occupancy; $60, double occupancy, including tour and plantation breakfast. No credit cards accepted. Children welcome. No pets. Swimming pool and antique shop on grounds.

DIRECTIONS: 35 miles north of Baton Rouge on US 61, 6 miles north of St. Francisville.

An English cottage in plantation country.

# ASPHODEL PLANTATION

Jackson

LOUISIANA

## A classic name for a classic plantation

Planter Benjamin Kendrick built this Greek Revival mansion in 1820 and turned to *The Odyssey* for the name: Homer spoke of an "Asphodel meadow of vast extent in the fields of Elysium." A decade was needed to finish construction, and during that time John James Audubon came to paint the portraits of Mr. Kendrick's daughter and her two sons. Asphodel was furnished with pieces purchased on trips to Europe, and many of these original furnishings can still be seen here today. During the Civil War, Union soldiers roamed the area in search of food. When they raided Asphodel, the mother and children locked themselves in the library until the soldiers left. It is said that a ghost from that frightening time still haunts the library.

Elsewhere on Asphodel's five hundred acres, about a mile from the mansion, is a small cluster of attractive buildings, most of them original. The Levy House pre-dates the mansion, and houses the inn, which has an excellent restaurant specializing in regional dishes: crabmeat Lorenzo, seafood gumbo, crayfish etoufée, and the traditional Monday fare in the area, red beans and rice. There are ten comfortable guest rooms across the way. A hearty breakfast and a tour of the plantation are included in the rates. The beautiful grounds invite leisurely walks through the woods.

ASPHODEL PLANTATION, Box 89, Jackson, LA 70748: (504) 654-6868; Mark Couhig, Innkeeper. A restored plantation with a complex of old and new buildings nearby. There are 10 guest rooms, including 4 suites, all with king-sized beds. Open all year except Christmas Eve and Christmas Day. Rates are $30, single occupancy; $50, double occupancy; $55 for a suite. A plantation breakfast and tour are included in the rates. The excellent dining room is open to the public for lunch and dinner. Children welcome ($7.50 charge over 14 years). Pets at the discretion of the innkeeper. On the spacious grounds are a swimming pool, two stocked ponds and nature trails. Gift shop.

DIRECTIONS: From Baton Rouge take US 61 north 12 miles to Rte. 68. North 8 miles to plantation.

Andrew Jackson visited here after winning the Battle of New Orleans.

# THE BURN

## A symbol of the wealth that once was Natchez

Before the Civil War, when cotton was king, Natchez was a city of incredible wealth, boasting thirteen bona fide millionaires. Prosperity ended with the war, but there remains a legacy: the single greatest collection of ante-bellum mansions in the South. Fifteen are open to the public throughout the year; during the March Pilgrimage the number rises to thirty.

An exceptional example of this architectural heritage is The Burn, built in 1832 by a Scotsman, John Walworth. Bound for New Orleans on a steamboat, Walworth got off at Natchez just to look around and decided to stay. His mansion is pure Greek Revival: four fluted Doric pilasters support the overhung second floor. Gardens surround the house, and among the flowers are one hundred and twenty-five varieties of camellias. Walworth, inspired by a lovely brook that ran through his property, named his home "The Burn," Scottish for "the brook." During the war, The Burn was appropriated by Federal troops who used it as their headquarters.

The Burn is completely furnished with antiques: beds by the master Prudent Mallard, Aubusson carpets, furniture carved by John Belter in the music room, Sevres porcelain, and a number of first-class eighteenth and nineteenth-century paintings. In the entrance hall is a semi-spiral, unsupported stairway that is a marvel of grace and engineering skill. A crystal chandelier hangs at the foot of the stairs.

The Burn was completely restored and opened for guests in 1978. Coincidentially, The Burn now is

owned by Tony Byrne, the mayor of Natchez, and his wife, Laveta, who also runs a restaurant in the old Natchez railroad station on the bluff overlooking the river. There is a guest suite in the main house, five others in the garçonnierre. (Most plantations and Southern mansions have garçonnierres, small dependencies were the sons of the owner could live with less parental supervision.) Each guest room has a private bath, television, and air conditioning. A sumptuous breakfast is served; dinner is available on request.

---

THE BURN, 712 North Union Street, Natchez, MS 39120; (601) 445-8566 or 442-1344; Lois Gore, Innkeeper. An ante-bellum Greek Revival mansion furnished to perfection. Open all year. Six guest rooms; 5 in the garçonnierre and one in main house. Rates: $65, single occupancy; $75, double occupancy, including full breakfast. MasterCard and Visa credit cards accepted. School age children only. No pets. Swimming pool on grounds.

DIRECTIONS: From downtown Natchez, State to Union Street, Union to The Burn (between B and Oak Street).

*Left.* The magnificent, unsupported staircase.

# MONMOUTH

## The mansion of "the most popular man in America"

Monmouth is a tribute to one man, John A. Quitman, who purchased it for his bride, Eliza, in 1826. (It had been built in 1818 by John Hankinson, who died an untimely death from yellow fever and is buried in a cemetery on the grounds.) Quitman had been governor of Mississippi, a congressman, and a hero-general of the Mexican War. His chambers, now a guest room, has a massive four-poster bed with a velvet-swagged testor, oriental carpeting, and a fireplace. It was in this room in 1858 that he died after a lingering illness caused, many say, by being poisoned at a banquet in honor of President Buchanan. At the time author Clayton Rand wrote, "John A. Quitman was the most popular man in all America." On display here is a gold sword presented to him by President Polk in honor of his bravery and leadership in battle. Other Quitman artifacts are his desk and the red handkerchief he used to rally his troops during the final assault on Mexico City.

Mr. and Mrs. Ronald Riches fell in love with Monmouth and Natchez while touring the South in 1979. Mr. Riches, a Los Angeles real estate developer, supervised the extensive restoration, which received the Restoration of the Year award from the state of Mississippi. Except for the Quitman bedroom, all eleven guest rooms are located in the former slave quarters, and all are beautifully appointed and wonderously comfortable with canopied beds, armoires, and the modern conveniences of air conditioning, cable television, and telephones. Breakfast is served in the original slave kitchen, completely furnished as it was one hundred and fifty years ago. The slave quarters also house an excellent collection of Civil War memorabilia: Confederate guns, swords, flags, maps, and many original letters written by Confederate leaders.

General Quitman's bedroom, now a guest room.

*Left.* The salon, showing the original furnishings throughout the inn.

MONMOUTH, Box 1736, Natchez, MS 39120; (601) 442-5852; Marguerite Guercio, Innkeeper. A beautifully restored and lavishly furnished 1818 mansion. Open all year. Eleven guest rooms, 2 in the mansion, 9 in restored slave quarters. Rates: $70, single occupancy; $75, double occupancy ($85 in mansion), including plantation breakfast and house tour. MasterCard and Visa credit cards accepted. Fishing pond on 26-acre grounds.
DIRECTIONS: From downtown Natchez, take State Street which becomes John A. Quitman Parkway. Monmouth is on the right just before parkway divides.

# LINDEN

## Happily, this didn't go with the wind

One of the oldest and most attractive mansions in Natchez is the Linden, built in 1790 on land granted in 1785 to Madam Sarah Truly by the King of Spain. It has been called "the Mount Vernon of the South," and its Federal Period façade does remind one of George Washington's Virginia home. Once owned by the first U.S. Senator from Mississippi, Linden has been in the Connors family since 1849. The present owner's children are the sixth generation of the family to live here. The house is in a setting of cedars and oaks festooned with Spanish moss. It is furnished by eighteenth and nineteenth-century pieces brought here by wealthy cotton planters: English furniture, French crystal, Chinese porcelain.

*Left.* The opulent dining room, with its punkah suspended over the table.

On a leisurely evening one can sit on the gallery at Linden, enjoy a cool drink and chat with the charming owner, Mrs. Jeanette Feltus, who knows all the stories worth telling about the house and Natchez. She will mention, of course, that Linden was one of the houses that appeared in the movie *Gone With The Wind.* One slips so easily into the ante-bellum mood it wouldn't be too surprising to see the Tarleton twins ride up.

LINDEN, Melrose Avenue, Natchez, MS 39120; (601) 445-5472; Jeanette Feltus, Innkeeper. Outstanding ante-bellum house in park-like setting. Open all year. Five guest suites. Rates: $60, single occupancy; $70 to $100, double occupancy. Full breakfast and tour included in rates. No credit cards accepted. Children over 14 years welcome. No pets.

DIRECTIONS: From downtown Natchez, State to Melrose Avenue then right to Linden.

## General Grant slept here

Vicksburg has the unfortunate distinction of being the only American city that was ever under seige, a testimony to its key role in the Civil War. The city, high on bluffs overlooking the Mississippi, could dominate the traffic on the river with its cannon, and it was the link with the Confederate states to the west. Abraham Lincoln once pointed to a map and said, "See what a lot of land these fellows hold, of which Vicksburg is the key. . . . Let us get Vicksburg and all that country is ours. The war can never be brought to a close unless that key is in our pocket."

Lincoln assigned the task to General Ulysses S. Grant. By mid-May 1863, Grant had seventy-one thousand men in front of the city; the entrenched Rebel forces numbered eighteen thousand. Frontal attacks were bloody but futile; more than five thousand men died. Forty-seven days of bombardment and starvation brought Vicksburg to its knees. Surrender came on the fourth of July—ironically, the same day Robert E. Lee turned in defeat from Gettysburg.

When Grant entered Vicksburg he chose Cedar Grove as his headquarters. His room with the original bed and furnishings is now a guest room—where else can one spend a night so immersed in American history? Cedar Grove had been shelled by Union gunboats during the seige, and a cannonball is still lodged in the door casing between the twin parlors.

Innkeeper Craig Gibson.

Cedar Grove was built by the Klein family from 1840 to 1858 in the popular Greek Revival style. Most of the original furnishings remain, including several monumental gold-leaf pier mirrors. Of particular interest are the books, silver, glassware, and china on display. Hoop-skirted young ladies give an enjoyable and informative house tour.

Cedar Grove now is owned by the Gibson family and young Craig Gibson is the manager. The four other guest rooms are themselves elegant and comfortable. A leisurely plantation breakfast is served in the dining room. A visit to Cedar Grove is a beautiful reminder of the quality of life enjoyed by the southern aristocracy before the war.

CEDAR GROVE, 2200 Oak Street, Vicksburg, MS 39180, (601) 636-1605; Craig R. Gibson, Innkeeper. Superb restoration of premier ante-bellum mansion. Open all year. Five guest rooms in main house. Rates: $75, double occupancy; $15 for each additional person in room. Rates include plantation breakfast in the formal dining room, house tour, and use of the sun parlor. MasterCard and Visa credit cards accepted. Children welcome. No pets.

DIRECTIONS: From downtown Vicksburg, toward river on Clay Street, south on Oak Street to Cedar Grove.

A guide shows off the family silver closet.

*Right.* Guests now sleep in General Grant's bed.

The salon, with original furnishings which are now antiques.

## A happy home;
## an exceptional inn

During the Civil War, Joseph Davis, brother of Jefferson Davis, moved here after the Union Army had burned his plantation, and the Confederate president himself once addressed the people of Vicksburg from the small second-story balcony. Originally built around 1830 by J.W. Mauldin, a member of the city's governing board, it was first a one-level wooden house. Ten years later, a "pretentious" front was put on the house with part of the original structure shaved off to accommodate it, and slave quarters were built of century-old brick at the rear.

*Left.* Antique furnishings in one of the guest rooms in the main house.

Now the mansion has been restored to its original magnificence by Mr. and Mrs. Martin White. Among its joys are exceptionally beautiful mirror staircases, and much of the original gas lighting.

Anchuca is the Choctaw word for "happy home"; it is a fitting choice for this inn. The master bedroom is a guest suite decorated in ante-bellum elegance at its highest. Five other rooms are in the former slave quarters, each decorated with taste and imagination. Guests are greeted with icy mint juleps served in elaborate silver mugs, the mint fresh from the garden. There is a sumptuous swimming pool and a hot tub in the cabana. Guests are unabashedly pampered, and those seeking a working definition of southern hospitality need look no further.

May White has spent six years looking for just the proper antique furnishings for Anchuca and her labors have been amply rewarded. It is hard to imagine the rooms looking any other way. Guests are free to roam the house at their leisure, a pleasant contrast to the ritualistic house tours at some southern mansions. A player piano in the library renders "Dixie" and Scott Joplin rags. For those with more auspicious musical credentials, a century-old Steinway in the parlor has exceptional tone and timbre.

Breakfast is served in the magnificence of the dining room: scrambled eggs, pancakes, particularly tasty cheese grits, hot biscuits, and steaming coffee.

Besides "happy home," Anchuca should have a second definition: one of the very best country inns to be found anywhere.

*Right.* A plantation breakfast is served amid the splendor of the formal dining room.

ANCHUCA, 1010 First East, Vicksburg, MS 39180; (601) 636-4931; Martin and May White, Innkeepers. Restored 1830 mansion with exceptional furnishings and guest accommodations. Open all year. Guest rooms: master suite in mansion and four rooms in restored slave quarters. Rates: $75 to $100, double occupancy ($5 less for single occupancy). Plantation breakfast and house tour included in rates. American Express, MasterCard and Visa credit cards accepted. Children welcome. No pets. Garden, swimming pool and whirlpool bath on grounds.

DIRECTIONS: I-20 exit 4B, down Clay to Cherry Street, right five blocks to First East.

Former slave quarters now are sumptuous guest rooms.

# MALAGA INN

## Twin townhouses joined by a garden

In 1862, when the South seemed to be winning the war, two merchants who were brothers-in-law built matching townhouses next door to each other on a tree-lined street near the bay. Their hopes and their fortunes suffered when Admiral David Farragut steamed his fleet into the bay on August 5, 1864, shouted "Damn the torpedoes! Full speed ahead!" and went on to win one of the bloodiest naval battles in history.

In 1979, the houses were acquired by Mayme Sinclair, a local realtor, who joined the houses by adding a center entrance and garden and created the Malaga Inn, named for Mobile's sister city in Spain. The guest rooms are attractively furnished with period furniture, and the restaurant serves up delicious regional specialities. The historical area around the inn is fascinating; the battleship *Alabama* is a mile away and the world-famed Bellingrath Gardens but a short drive.

*Left:* Mobile's wonderfully colorful Bellingrath Gardens are just a short drive from the inn.

MALAGA INN, 359 Church Street, Mobile, AL 36602; (205) 438-4701; Mayme Sinclair, Innkeeper. Twin townhouses joined by a courtyard and a veranda-fronted wing. Open all year. Forty-one rooms ranging in price from $36, single occupancy, to $92 suites, all with private bath and period furnishings. Dining room is open to the public 3 meals a day (continental breakfast only on Sunday). Children welcome. Pets at the discretion of the innkeeper. American Express, Diners Club, MasterCard and Visa credit cards accepted. Swimming pool. Public golf and tennis courts nearby. Deep sea fishing and sailing available in the area.

DIRECTIONS: I-65 south to Rte. 90 (Government Street), or east-west I-10 to Canal Street exit, then Canal to Rte. 90. Right on Clairborne Street to Church Street. Inn is at the corner.

The twin townhouses, preserved complete with their ornate iron balconies.

# A hotel that earns its name every day

A grand hotel must meet some exacting standards. The setting must be exquisite, the accommodations sumptuous, the service impeccable. The dining room must be excellent, but that isn't enough. The food must be presented with flair, guests must dress for dinner, there must be dancing later to a live orchestra, the emphasis on fox trots and waltzes. There must be an excellent golf course with a club house, ample tennis courts, an outsized swimming pool. You must be able to shoot skeet, rent a bicycle or a sailboat. There must be shops in the lobby offering resort fashions. There must be a putting green on the lawn. Old employees must remember your name. Your bed must be turned down for you at night, a bit of chocolate wrapped in gold foil on your pillow. There must be Postum on the menu.

The Grand Motel at Point Clear passes all these tests with flying colors, and goes beyond. There is a fifty-two-foot Hatteras sport fisherman for charter and the kitchen will clean and prepare your catch for you. Waiter Bucky Miller has been at the hotel for nearly forty years and has a memory for names that rivals that of the late Jim Farley. Bucky has a mint patch in the garden outside the Bird Cage Lounge; when you order a mint julep he picks the mint expressly for you.

Mobile Bay is one of two places in the world where a strange phenomenon called a "jubilee" regularly occurs. On a summer's night thousands and thousands of fish and shellfish will suddenly—without warning or explanation—come up on the beach. A jubilee is usually confined to a section of a hundred yards or so but may occur anywhere around the bay. Residents take turns watching for the fish and when they're spotted the alarm is sounded, people rush to the beach, baskets are filled with fish and a spontaneous celebration is underway.

*Left.* Bucky Miller standing in front of his mint garden with one of his famous mint juleps.

The sunny dining room overlooks the lawn and beach.

The Grand Hotel recently was acquired by Marriott, an event which gave many of the long-time guests pause. But the only changes to date have been for the good and the Grand Hotel, which began operation in 1847, looks forward to a rosy future.

*Warning to golfers:* There is an alligator in residence in the lagoon beside the fairway on the ninth hole.

GRAND HOTEL, Point Clear, AL 36564, (205) 928-9201, William Scott, General Manager. A resort hotel in the grand tradition since 1847, now operated by the Marriott Corp., offering 172 guest accommodations in hotel and nearby cottages. Open all year. Rates $58 to $102 per room European Plan; Modified American Plan available at $24 per person additional. Dining room open to public 3 meals a day. Children welcome. No pets. American Express, Diners Club, MasterCard and Visa credit cards accepted. Full resort facilities including 27-hole golf course, 10 tennis courts, sailboats, ski boats, charter deep sea fishing yacht, bicycles, lawn sports.

DIRECTIONS: Hotel is 23 miles southeast of Mobile on US 98, off I-10.

The back of the hotel overlooks the beach, *right,* and a putting green.

# CHATTANOOGA CHOO-CHOO

Chattanooga

**TENNESSEE**

## The glory that was American railroading

When the Southern Railway opened the Terminal Station in 1909, it was acclaimed as one of the most beautiful depots in the world. Understandably so. Architect Donn Barber's plans had won first prize in the Paris Beaux Arts Competition before being purchased by the railroad. The magnificent station saw the glory days of American railroading, but when rail travel through Chattanooga was discontinued in 1970, it was left to fall into disrepair. Fortunately, a group of twenty-four local businessmen raised the funds necessary for restoration and, in 1973, it reopened as a stunning complex of shops, restaurants, lounges, acres of formal gardens, Hilton Motor Inn, an ice

*Left.* The old Southern Railway terminal houses the public rooms of the inn.

skating rink, tennis courts, swimming pool, and enough reminders of the Age of Steam to keep a railroad buff happy for days. Behind the station is a beautifully restored 1880 wood-burning engine and tender (Glenn Miller devotees will note that it is on Track 29 and that there is a shoeshine stand nearby).

Twenty-four vintage Pullman sleeping cars have been transformed into forty-eight Victorian suites with red carpeting, flocked wallpaper, and inviting king-sized brass beds. Near the swimming pool is a domed blue-and-silver car that houses a suite named after Harry Warren, composer of "The Chattanooga Choo-Choo." It houses a parlor complete with wet bar and a Jacuzzi in the dome. There is a club car, of course, named The Wabash Cannonball, and a dining car, Le Grand Diner, where one can enjoy a superb eight-course French dinner in Victorian splendor while fantasizing about the Orient Express. In the station, the former waiting room and main lobby

The Grand Dome restaurant is one of three in the inn.

is now The Grand Dome restaurant, and the eighty-five-foot dome, the largest unsupported dome in the world, is truly a sight to behold. In what was the Railway Express office is The Station House restaurant, less formal, with a Dixieland jazz band most evenings. Also in the station is one of the world's largest and most elaborate model railroads, one hundred and seventy-five feet from end to end, covering more than three thousand square feet. The working HO system includes models of the city's Terminal and Union stations. The Chattanooga Choo-Choo complex covers twenty-four acres, and there are two antique trolley cars to shuttle guests to the various points of interest.

The Chattanooga Choo-Choo stretches the definition of a country inn a bit, but it more than compensates for this transgression by being such good fun.

*Right.* A restored 1880 woodburning 4-4-0 locomotive on display at the inn.

CHATTANOOGA CHOO-CHOO, Terminal Station, 1400 Market St., Chattanooga, TN 37402; (615) 266-5000; B.A. Casey, Jr., President. Once a Beaux Arts railroad station, now a Hilton hotel complex with 375 rooms including 48 suites in restored Pullman cars. Open all year. Rates $45 to $80, double occupancy; $65 for the Pullman suites, other suites to $500. Four public restaurants: Palm Terrace and Grand Dome in main station seating 1,000, Station House with cabaret entertainment, the Trolley Cafe by the swimming pool and the private dining car, Le Grande. In warm weather the Trellis Bar & Grill serves light meals. Children are welcome at no extra charge when accompanied by parents; no facilities for pets. American Express, Diners Club, Carte Blanche, MasterCard and Visa credit cards accepted. Indoor and outdoor swimming pools, tennis courts, formal gardens, antique trolley car touring the 24-acre complex, and world's largest model railroad.

DIRECTIONS: I-24 to Market Street exit—station is six blocks from downtown Chattanooga; from Nashville take Lookout Mountain-Broad Street exit and follow signs.

Pullman cars have been converted into luxurious suites.

# REELFOOT LAKE INN

Tiptonville              **TENNESSEE**

## Fishing, duck hunting and bald eagles

If the lake wasn't so lovely and the recreational facilities so ample, this inn should carry the disclaimer "For Sportsmen Only." The fishing is splendid, yielding up catfish, bass, blue gill, and crappie in copious numbers. The forty-five-day duck season in the fall lures hunters from a half-dozen states. And in the winter, Reelfoot Lake is home to more than two hundred American bald eagles, an endangered species rarely seen this far east. Some twelve thousand people come here each year to see our national bird in its native habitat.

This is a state park, and the state built the inn in 1973. The inn and the lodging units are all built on poles in the lake and connected by elevated walkways; it gives one the feeling of being on a commodious houseboat, except that it doesn't rock. Across the way a small airport caters to the private pilot.

REELFOOT LAKE AIRPARK INN, Rte. 1, Box 296, Tiptonville, TN 38079; (901) 253-7756; Ralph Burrus, Innkeeper. State-owned lodges and inn on beautiful lake in Northeast Tennessee. Open all year. Twelve accommodations in 5 lodges, all with private baths. Rates: $32 for two persons, double occupancy, $6 per additional person; $44 for four persons. Dining room open to public 3 meals a day; no liquor served or allowed. MasterCard and Visa credit cards accepted. Children welcome; pet permitted on leash. Excellent fishing and duck hunting during 45-day late fall season. Swimming pool, small boat rental, facilities for private planes at adjacent airport. From December to March, Reelfoot Lake is home to 200 American Bald Eagles.

DIRECTIONS: 51 miles north of Memphis. US 51 north to Dyersburg, west 2 miles to Rte. 78 north to Tiptonville. Inn is 8 miles north of town just east of Rte. 78.

One of the duplex guest houses built right on the lake.

Innkeepers Roll and Wilma Maples.

## The wonders of nature, the crafts of man

Nowhere does nature present a more lovely or more intriguing face to man than in the mountains called the Great Smokies. This range, the ancestral home of the Cherokees, is breathtakingly beautiful, whether viewed from the 6,642-foot peak of Clingmans Dome or the serenity of Cades Cove. The half-million acre national park is a mecca for those who love wild flowers, wildlife, or simply the majesty of unspoiled scenery.

Roll Maples grew up in the Smokies; his father delivered mail on horseback there. After the national park was created in 1934 and the government had bought the family farm, he moved to nearby Gatlinburg and built the Gatlinburg Inn in 1937. He and his wife still run it and under their careful supervision it has built a reputation for comfort and charm that is unmatched in the area. The inn is an ideal base from which to explore the Smokies or the myriad of excellent craft shops of Gatlinburg.

GATLINBURG INN, 755 Parkway, Gatlinburg, TN 37738; (615) 436-5133; Roll and Wilma Maples, Innkeepers. A rambling stone inn, built in 1937, offering 67 guest accommodations, all with color TV and private baths. Open April 1 to October 31. Rates $48 to $55, double occupancy; suites to $135. No meals served but excellent restaurants nearby. No credit cards accepted. Swimming pool, tennis courts, shuffleboard, and children's playground on premises. About 1 mile from entrance to Great Smokies National Park.

DIRECTIONS: From Knoxville, I-40 east to US 441 south, 25 miles to Gatlinburg.

A guest room showing a quilt made by Mrs. Maples.

OVERLEAF. View of Tennessee's Great Smokies.

Memphis # PEABODY HOTEL **TENNESSEE**

## A *grand luxe* hotel with personality

*There are Mississippians who believe that when they die, heaven will be like the Peabody lobby.*
ANONYMOUS, CIRCA 1940

Precisely at seven each morning a red carpet is rolled out from the elevator bank to the ornate marble fountain in the center of the Peabody lobby. Liveried bellmen stand at attention, and the guests crowd around. A Sousa march comes over the public address system. The elevator doors open; six ducks waddle along the carpet and hop up into the fountain. The guests applaud, acting out their part in a fifty-year-old tradition. At three in the afternoon, the ducks ceremoniously make their way to the elevator where they are whisked to their home on the hotel's roof.

The Peabody *is* tradition and has exerted an almost mystic hold on the imagination of the area since it was built in 1869. A new Peabody was opened in 1925, its glory a two-story Italian Renaissance Revival

*Left.* The famous ducks in the lobby fountain.

lobby and the fountain, carved from a single block of Travertine marble.

Hard times fell on the Peabody after World War II. It went up for auction in 1964, was acquired by the Sheraton chain, then closed again. In 1975 it was acquired by the Belz family, the state's largest developers, and restored to perfection.

Today the Peabody is once again a member in good standing in that most exclusive society: the *grand luxe* hotels with personalities all their own. Anyone wishing to savor the flavor of the South should make the Peabody a must stop.

THE PEABODY, 149 Union Street, Memphis, TN 38103; (901) 529-4000; Hans Demuth, General Manager. The city's premier hotel, its 452 rooms and public areas beautifully restored to past glory. Open all year. Rates: $55, single; $95, double; suites to $350. Two restaurants: Chez Phillippe, serving classic French cuisine, and the popularly priced Dux. Breakfast is also served in the main lobby. Children are welcome. No pets. Hotel has gift shop, indoor swimming pool, and health club with sauna, steamroom, and whirlpool. World famous for the daily parade of ducks that swim in the lobby fountain.

DIRECTIONS: The Peabody is in the heart of downtown Memphis.

They don't make grand hotel lobbies like they used to.

# WILLIAMS HOUSE INN

## The waters are healthful, the food delicious

Babe Ruth was a frequent visitor in Hot Springs. So was Al Capone. Both liked the combination of healing waters and wide-open gambling. The gambling was shut down in the 1950s but visitors still come for the waters and the recreational facilities in this, the only American city entirely within a national park.

Mary and Gary Riley are Iowans who lived in Saudi Arabia and California before settling here and becoming innkeepers. They bought an 1889 Victorian mansion that was built by a Boston doctor. A disastrous fire in 1913 nearly demolished the Williams house but the doctor, a six-foot-six giant of a man, hastily organized a bucket brigade, albeit with the help of a shotgun, and saved all the house except for a bit of gingerbread.

The house is charmingly furnished with Victoriana, the guest rooms are inviting, and one makes the happy discovery that Mary is a first-rate cook. Although basically a bed and breakfast establishment, box lunches and dinners may be had on request.

WILLIAMS HOUSE INN, 420 Quapaw Avenue, Hot Springs, AR 71901; (501) 624-4275, Gary and Mary Riley, Innkeepers. Victorian doctor's home converted into attractive guest house. Open all year. Five guest rooms. Rates: $35 to $55, double occupancy; $5 less for single occupancy. Rates include an excellent breakfast. Dinner may be had by special arrangement. No credit cards accepted. School age children welcome. No pets. Three blocks from Bathhouse Row.

DIRECTIONS: From downtown Hot Springs, take Central Avenue (Bathouse Row) south to Prospect then right on Orange to inn.

# Eureka Springs DAIRY HOLLOW HOUSE ARKANSAS

## A dairy maid serves a breakfast to remember

Crescent Dragonwagon, who writes children's books, her husband, a restoration consultant, and their partner, Bill Haymes, bought this diminutive ninety-year-old farmhouse in 1979 and turned it into an oasis of easy charm. There are only two guest rooms, the Rose Room and the Iris Room, color coordinated to fit their names. The twin beds in the Iris Room have quilts with the Bear's Paw and Goose Tracks patterns; the Rose Room's double-bed quilt is, appropriately, the Dutch Rose pattern. The Rose Bath has an out-sized clawfoot tub, and a skylight; the Iris Bath has a shower and an intricate tile floor.

A pleasant walk from town, the house is in a quiet valley, once the preserve of dairy farms. The path to the house is through a well-tended flower garden. Breakfast is a particular treat, prepared by a "dairymaid" who arrives magically in the morning. Coffee, tea, herb tea, or café au lait may be taken in one's room, followed by a goblet of wonderously fresh orange juice. Next, a basket of fresh-baked butterhorns and a loaf of sweet bread, or a puffy and golden German baked pancake. Homemade jams and fresh butter complete the feast.

---

DAIRY HOLLOW HOUSE, Box 221, Eureka Springs, AR 72632; (501) 253-7444; Carole McLearen, Innkeeper. Two guest rooms in beautifully converted farmer's cottage. Open all year. Rates: $49, double occupancy, weekdays; $59, weekends; $5 less for single occupancy. (Midweek, 3-5 days, $39 per day, double occupancy.) Rates include exceptional breakfast. School age children welcome. No pets. American Express, MasterCard and Visa credit cards accepted.

DIRECTIONS: From Little Rock, northwest on I-40 to Conway, US 65 to US 62 to Eureka Springs. Dairy Hollow is a few minutes drive from town: Spring Street past the Post Office one mile, then follow signs.

Innkeeper Crescent Dragonwagon, center, and her two dairy maids.

# CRESCENT HOTEL

Eureka Springs      **ARKANSAS**

## A Victorian grand hotel makes a comeback

High atop West Mountain, overlooking the ginger-bread houses of the town, a massive Gothic hotel was built in 1886 to house the people who flocked here for the healing springs. The waters lost their appeal around the turn of the century and the Crescent had to improvise to stay alive. In the winters it housed a girl's school, the Crescent College and Conservancy, and took in conventional guests in the summer. The school vanished in the Depression and a cancer quack made the hotel his clinic. The good doctor kept loaded machine guns in his office, but he eventually was arrested and imprisoned for fraud. Restoration began on the Crescent in the late 1940s, and today it is spick and span, bustling with a new-found vigor.

*Left.* The Crescent Hotel, overlooking Eureka Springs.

The lobby is of heroic proportions with a grand stone fireplace. The Crystal Dining Room has a wall of imposingly tall windows and crystal chandeliers. There is the "Top of the Crescent" lounge on the roof with a spectacular view. The rooms all have been refurbished and echo the hotel's insistence on Victorian comfort. On the hotel's twenty-seven acres are gardens, woodland paths, and the mandatory swimming pool and tennis court.

CRESCENT HOTEL, 75 Prospect Street, Eureka Springs, AR 72632; (501) 253-9766; Jerry Hope, Innkeeper. An 1886 hotel on a hilltop overlooking Victorian mountain town. Open all year. Seventy-six restored guest rooms. Rates: $32 to $70, double occupancy, $3 per additional person in room. Breakfast, lunch and dinner served in Crystal Room. (In off-season, meals served in Crescent Springs Restaurant only.) American Express, MasterCard and Visa credit cards accepted. Children and pets welcome. Swimming pool, tennis court, and shuffleboard. Dancing in Crystal Room every evening except Sunday.

DIRECTIONS: From Little Rock, northwest on I-40 to Conway, US 65 to US 62 to Eureka Springs. Hotel is 8 blocks north of center of town on US 62 (business).

Cecil Walker, assistant manager of the Crescent, where time seems to stand still.

# NEW ORLEANS HOTEL

Eureka Springs     **ARKANSAS**

## A joyously unconventional place for a holiday

In the late Victorian era well-to-do families needed a proper reason to take a summer vacation. The spiritual uplift of a Chautauqua meeting would do very nicely, or the physical well-being induced by water from mineral springs. This town of gingerbread houses and winding streets came into being practically overnight to cater to those attracted by its waters and clear mountain air—most every building dates from the late 1880s. With the coming of the twentieth century, Americans decided that fun was sufficient excuse for a holiday, and Eureka Springs fell into a sleep as profound as that of Brigadoon.

Hippies discovered the town in the early 1960s. The residents were scandalized but the new arrivals were soon a respectable, if colorful, part of the scene, more intent on arts and crafts then on more dangerously aberrant behavior. Everyone here now seems to have come from somewhere else, and everyone professes a love for Eureka Springs and the life it represents. A visitor soon understands why.

Among the new people here are Phil and Florence Schloss, who own and operate the New Orleans Hotel. Phil, a retired Marine colonel and former Chicago advertising executive, has been restoring the century-old hotel, room by room, since 1976. The lobby has a ceiling of pressed tin, an antique nickel cash register is at the desk, and Victorian furniture groupings break up the large area. The lobby and the façade, with the decorative ironwork on the balconies that suggest New Orleans, were seen in a recent movie on public television, "Belle Starr." The twenty-two rooms are pleasant, with all the conveniences except telephone or television. Each room is different from the other, representing the eclectic nature of the Schlosses' antique acquisitions. Off the lobby is an unpretentious restaurant managed by the town's mayor and her husband. It is as much a local watering hole and political clubhouse as it is a restaurant. The food is excellent, however, and on Thursday nights a pound of freshly boiled shrimp will be served up for under five dollars. On the level below the lobby

The vintage bus provides visitors with a ride around the town.

is another restaurant, The Quarter, offering, among more substantial dishes, sixteen varieties of hamburger. Live music is offered most nights. The Ukulele Club of Eureka Springs meets Saturday nights in the lobby for a sing-along. For fine, gourmet dining, The Palace restaurant is just a short walk away. All in all, a joyously unconventional place for a holiday.

---

NEW ORLEANS HOTEL, 63 Spring Street, Eureka Springs, AR 72632; (501) 253-8630; Phil and Flo Schloss, Innkeepers. Victorian hotel in the heart of picturesque mountain community. Open all year. Twenty-two guest rooms, including 4 parlor suites. Rates: $30 to $44, double occupancy; less off-season (December 1 to March 31). French Market off the lobby open to public serving three meals a day, except Sunday; The Quarter, an informal bistro, open to public for lunch and dinner, except Sunday, and often has live entertainment. No credit cards accepted. Children welcome at no charge. Pets welcome.

DIRECTIONS: From Little Rock, northwest on I-40 to Conway, Rte. 65 to US 62 to Eureka Springs. Hotel is on main business street.

*Left.* Photographed at The Palace, a fine restaurant just a few blocks from the hotel.

# Mountain View OZARK FOLK CENTER ARKANSAS

## Thar's talent in them thar hills!

From May 1st to October 31st each year, visitors flock here by the thousands to enjoy the multi-faceted talents of the people of the Ozarks. The state has built an eighty-acre entertainment complex to serve as "a living museum of mountain heritage, crafts and music." Twenty small buildings house demonstrations of the so-called cabin crafts: basketry, quilt-making, woodcarving, and the like. From Memorial Day to Labor Day there is a musical show each night (except Mondays) that is worth the trip all by itself. This is not commercial country and western but the authentic songs and dances of these hardy mountaineers, and it's a joy. Guests find themselves joining in the square dances and loving it.

Adjacent to the center is the lodge, a cluster of thirty attractive duplex cabins. The accommodations

*Left.* Ozark musicians provide daily mountain music for listening and square dancing.

are more like suites than ordinary rooms. As well as hiking trails, there is a swimming pool and a restaurant that does a good job with such southern specialities as country ham and chicken and dumplings.

Of particular interest is the gift shop and its array of reasonably priced, first-class craft merchandise. One finds the absence of shoddy goods a refreshing change from the shops at so many tourist attractions.

OZARK FOLK CENTER LODGE, Box 500, Mountain View, AR 72560; (501) 269-3871; June Burroughs, Innkeeper. Sixty attractive rooms in modern cabins next to state Folk Center complex. Open all year. (Folk Center is open May 1 through October 31.) Rooms can accommodate up to four adults. Rates: $34, double occupancy, $3 per additional person. Children under 13 no charge. Restaurant in center open to public, three meals a day. Children and pets welcome. Special events: Annual Arkansas Folk Festival, last two weekends in April; National Fiddlers Competition, first weekend in November; Annual Ozark Christmas Festival, second weekend in December. MasterCard and Visa credit cards accepted. Swimming pool, recreation room, and hiking trail.

DIRECTIONS: From Little Rock, US 67 north to Bald Knob, US 167 north toward Batesville. West on Rte. 14 to Mountain View.

Modern guest cottages are part of the inn's facilities.

# Mountain View INN AT MOUNTAIN VIEW ARKANSAS

## The nostalgia of yesteryear

In this quaint little town is a quaint little inn that reminds one how nice it must have been to live in a place like this a hundred years ago. The inn was built as a house in the early 1880s, became an inn in 1886, and has been one ever since. The inn has nine rooms and, one can be sure, is one of the few places in the country where a room can be had for eighteen dollars. A family style, stick-to-your-ribs breakfast—scrambled eggs, sausage and gravy, biscuits, juice, and coffee—will cost you another three dollars. The inn is presided over by Karen Jackson. Also in evidence is a chow who looks for all the world like Bert Lahr as the cowardly lion in *The Wizard of Oz*.

THE INN AT MOUNTAIN VIEW, Box 86, Mountain View, AR 72560; (501) 269-4200; Karen Jackson, Innkeeper. A century-old Victorian house in a sleepy Arkansas village. Open all year. Eleven guest rooms, most with shared bath. Rates: $18, single occupancy, to $30, double occupancy with private bath; $3 charge for additional person. Juice and coffee included in rates. Country breakfast served family style, $3. No credit cards accepted.

DIRECTIONS: From Little Rock, US 67 north to Bald Knob, US 167 north toward Batesville. West on Rte. 14 to Mountain View.

*Right*. A working Chandler & Price platen press, one of the many exhibits at the crafts center. OVERLEAF. Historic Elkhorn Tavern, the subject of a recent historical novel which describes the Pea Ridge, Arkansas, Civil War battle that raged around the tavern. Some of the guns used are still in place. On the right is the charming sign of the inn following.

An inn for almost a hundred years.

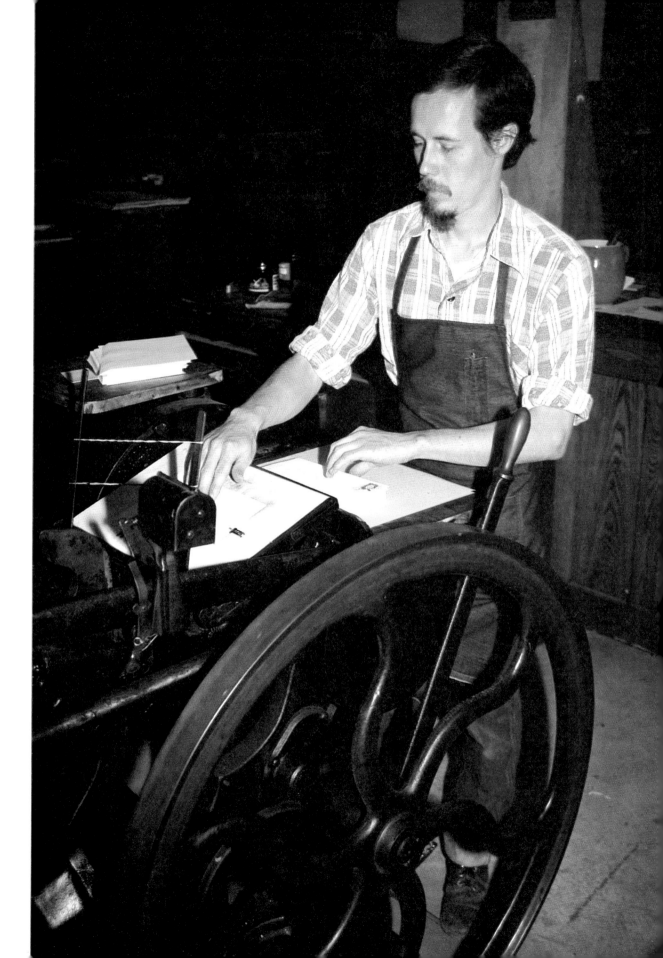

Inn Ste. Gemme Beauvais

Welcome

Dolly Dufour

# Sainte Genevieve STE. GEMME BEAUVAIS

## Old France flourished on the Mississippi

Sainte Genevieve was the first permanent white settlement in the state. It already was a thriving community when the first settlers arrived at what is now St. Louis. Nearly all of the thirty buildings erected here before 1800 are still standing and in good repair, and many are inhabited by direct descendents of the original French owners. Each August thousands of visitors flock to this unusual community for the *Jour de Fête à Ste. Genevieve.*

"Boats" Donze grew up in the house that is now the inn. He and his wife Frankye purchased it in 1973 and after extensive restoration it is now a lovely Victorian inn. It was built in 1848 on part of the Beauvais estate and, over the years, has alternated from private home to boarding house. During Prohibition, recalls "Boats," the basement contained the busiest speakeasy between St. Louis and Cape Girardeau. There are eight spacious guest rooms, and a handsome dining room offering breakfast (and lunch during the summer). Sainte Genevieve has a singular charm, and a leisurely inspection of its architectural treasures will reward the visitor.

INN STE. GEMME BEAUVAIS, 78 North Main Street, Ste. Genevieve, MO 63670; (314) 883-5744; Boats and Frankye Donze, Innkeepers. An 1848 house in oldest White settlement west of Mississippi converted to intimate inn. Open all year. Eight guest rooms, including one suite, mostly furnished with antiques, some with private baths. Rates $35, double occupancy, $15 for additional person in room. Rates include full breakfast. MasterCard accepted. Children welcome ($6 charge under 12 years). No pets.

DIRECTIONS: From St. Louis, south on I-55 to Bloomsdale exit; Rte. 32 (Fourth Street) to 4-way stop, right 3 blocks to inn.

| Lesterville | # WILDERNESS LODGE | **MISSOURI** |
|---|---|---|

## Horses, hayrides and a treehouse for the kids

If it's possible to rough it in comfort, one certainly can do it here. Cabins, individual and multiple-unit, are carefully situated around the grounds to give guests the feeling of splendid isolation. The lodge serves up hearty breakfasts and dinners and packs lunches for those off for canoe trips, trail rides, or fishing. The recreational facilities include just about everything from archery and bocce to regular and platform tennis—there's even a children's playground complete with treehouse. Moonlight hayrides are a weekly feature. Stables are a short walk away and the Wilderness Lodge seems to attract more than its share of equestrians.

The tree house is of more interest to the younger guests.

WILDERNESS LODGE, Box 90, Lesterville, MO 63654; (314) 637-2295; Sue Crawford, Innkeeper. Family resort in lovely Ozark setting. Twenty-seven guests rooms in attractive cottages, including 4 individual cottages, most with fireplaces. Open all year. Rates in season (May 1 to September 30) $48.50 to $59, double occupancy; off-season, $41.50 to $53. (Special off-season packages available.) Rates include breakfast and dinner in family-style dining room. (Open to public by reservation.) American Express, Diners Club, MasterCard and Visa credit cards accepted. Children welcome. No pets. Tennis, private beach, canoes, horseback riding nearby, excellent fishing in Black River.

DIRECTIONS: From St. Louis, I-55 to US 67 south to Fredericktown. West on Rte. 72 to Lesterville, Two miles east to gravel road, follow signs 2 miles to lodge.

# Saint Louis CHESHIRE INN & LODGE MISSOURI

## A bit of England in jolly old Saint Louis

This is an Anglophile's dream come true—a Tudor inn filled with English antiques and run with British care and precision, next door to a lovely park and ten minutes from downtown St. Louis. The Inn, actually, is a restaurant; the Lodge is where one stays. Many of the rooms are named for English authors—Fielding, Johnson, Dickens, and the like—and contain canopied beds so high one must use a stepladder to retire. In the lobby is a bookcase of old editions of English classics that guests may borrow should they wish to pursue the Old England illusion a step further.

The inn serves up traditional British fare: the prime ribs of beef, with Yorkshire pudding and a dash of horseradish sauce, is fit for at least a lord of the realm. It is a St. Louis tradition to dine here before a sporting event, then be taken there and back by one of the Cheshire's double-decker London buses. If that seems a bit too plebian, there is a 1962 Silver Cloud Rolls-Royce and chauffeur for hire.

The Cheshire delivers complimentary orange juice and coffee to your room in the morning. This is but a prelude to the breakfast that is served from seven to ten on weekdays, a buffet with all the usual delights and such specialities as chicken Cantonese, prime-rib hash, fried bananas and chicken livers.

Not the least of it is that the Cheshire's prices are most reasonable. To come to St. Louis and not stay here would be . . . well, a bloody shame.

---

CHESHIRE INN & LODGE, 6300 Clayton Road, St. Louis, MO 63117; (314) 647-7300; (toll free from out of state, 1-800 325-7378); Jim Prentice, General Manager. English Tudor style hotel complex next to Forest Park. Open all year. Lodge has 110 guest accommodations, including 10 suites. Rates $52 to $70, single occupancy, suites $105. Rates include orange juice and coffee. Inn serves gourmet quality roast beef and steaks (closed New Year's Day, Memorial Day, July 4th and Christmas). Light lunches at the King's Arms in inn, Monday to Friday. American Express, Diners Club, MasterCard and Visa credit cards accepted. Children welcome (crib: $2). No pets. Swimming pool, co-ed spa (adults only, no charge), transportation on double-decker buses to sporting and cultural events.

DIRECTIONS: From downtown St. Louis, I-40W to Clayton exit.

Manager Tony Bouaoun with the lodge's Silver Cloud Rolls Royce.

# DOE RUN INN

Brandenburg **KENTUCKY**

## A historic treasure on the old frontier

In the hills of western Kentucky, near the gold bullion reserves of Fort Knox, lies a treasure of an altogether different sort: an inn that traces its origins to the time when this was the American frontier, the western edge of our civilization. Squire Boone, brother to the legendary Daniel, discovered the brook and named it Doe Run for the deer and elk that drank from its clear-running waters. He claimed the land around Doe Run in 1786; the deed was signed by Patrick Henry, governor of Virginia, as the area was then Little York, part of Virginia. Around 1800, construction began on the building that is now the inn. Abraham Lincoln's father, Thomas, worked here as a stone mason.

First a woolen mill, then a grist mill and flour mill, Doe Run was made into an inn in 1927 by Wash Coleman, whose great-granddaughter, Lucille Brown, now owns and operates the inn with her husband, Curtis. The Browns have preserved many of the antique furnishings: the second-floor Honeymoon Room has a one-hundred-and-fifty-year-old hand-made walnut bed, and in the hallway nearby is a solid cherry chest that was brought down the Ohio River by packet boat before the Civil War. A massive oak standing desk in the lobby was used by the original mill owners.

The big lobby, dominated by a grand, stone fireplace, is warm and inviting. There is a dining room, but in warm weather meals are served on a long screened-in porch overlooking the brook. The simple country fare is hearty and delicious: southern fried chicken with cream gravy and hot biscuits, fried Kentucky country ham with red-eye gravy, steaks or fresh fish, topped off by Mrs. Brown's speciality, a melt-in-the-mouth lemon pie made from a closely guarded family recipe. Local laws permit only beer to be served but guests may bring their own wine or liquor.

There are twenty-two rooms at Doe Run. Only a few have private baths, but all are furnished with originality and charm. The inn's one thousand acres

Guest rooms are furnished with a variety of antiques.

offer miles of paths through woods little changed since the time of Squire Boone. The brook is stocked with enough Rainbow trout to satisfy even the most ardent fisherman.

The Doe Run Inn is a sanctuary in a noisy world. It is not for those travelers who confuse luxury with comfort, but rather for the discerning who seek original treasures.

DOE RUN INN, Rte. 2, Brandenburg, KY 40108; (502) 422-9982; Curtis and Lucille Brown, Innkeepers. A pre-Revolutionary mill converted into an 18-room inn. Open all year. Rates $18 (shared bath), $22 (private bath), double occupancy. Dining room, serving southern specialities, open to public for 3 meals a day (closed Christmas Eve and Christmas Day); beer only, guests may bring liquor. Children welcome; no pets. MasterCard and Visa credit cards accepted. Hiking and Rainbow Trout fishing on grounds. Public swimming pool and 18-hole golf course 2 miles away.

DIRECTIONS: On US 31W, south from Louisville to Muldraugh, west on Rte. 1638 to Brandenburg, south 4 miles to inn.

*Left.* The inn takes its name from the stream beside it.

# OLD TALBOTT TAVERN

Bardstown      KENTUCKY

## Jesse James, the Lincolns and the Prince of France

Old Talbott Tavern, the first hostelry west of the Alleghenies, has been in continuous operation since 1779. During the Revolution, the building was used to store munitions and supplies for General George Rogers Clark and his troops. Later it was the western terminus of the stagecoach road from Philadelphia and Virginia. Among the Talbott guests in the early years: Andrew Jackson, Henry Clay, William Henry Harrison, Zackery Taylor, Stephen Foster and John J. Audubon. Young Abraham Lincoln stayed here with his parents and family during a court trial in which they attempted to establish ownership of their farm. The Lincolns lost and moved west. Prince Louis Phillippe, later King of France, spent part of

*Left.* Men of the frontier have stopped here for meals since 1799.

his year of exile here. Members of his party painted French countryside scenes on the walls of several of the upstairs rooms. A guest got into a fracas some years later and marred the wall paintings with bullet holes. He is best remembered by his assumed name: Jesse James.

OLD TALBOTT TAVERN INN, Stephen Foster Blvd., Bardstown, KY 40403; (502) 348-3494; Johnny and Peggy Downs, Innkeepers. One of the oldest hotels west of the Alleghenies, the Talbott has been in continuous operation since 1779. There are 5 guest rooms with period furnishings, all with private baths. Open all year. Rates $28 to $38, double occupancy. Dining room, offering southern specialities, is open to the public for lunch and dinner. Children welcome (no charge under 12 years); no facilities for pets. Public tennis courts and swimming pool two blocks away. An outdoor theatre in Bardstown presents the "Stephen Foster Story" each summer. The house that inspired Foster's "My Old Kentucky Home" is nearby and open to the public.

DIRECTIONS: US 31E, 30 miles south of Louisville, or exit 25 off the Blue Grass Parkway from Lexington.

# BOONE TAVERN HOTEL

## Southern hospitality with a college education

The Boone Tavern Hotel is part of a unique educational institution, Berea College, which was founded in 1859 by abolitionists seeking to give "an education to all colors, classes, cheap and thorough." Although forced to close down during the Civil War, Berea College has fulfilled its promise ever since. The college has a special commitment to the Appalachian region—many of the students elect to study the native crafts of weaving, quilting, basketry, carving and furniture making, and their products are deservedly famous.

The Georgian-style hotel was built as a college guest house in 1909, in part by student labor. Now its fifty-nine rooms are full most of the year, in large measure by visitors drawn to Berea by the rich panoply of crafts. Students on the college work program comprise much of the staff at both the hotel and its excellent dining room.

BOONE TAVERN HOTEL, Main Street, Berea, KY 40403; (606) 986-9341, Ext. 200; Curtis Reppert, General Manager. A handsome brick Georgian hotel built in 1909 by Berea College. Open all year. Offers 59 rooms decorated with furniture built by students. Rates: $19 to $34, single occupancy; $25 to $42, double occupancy. Southern specialities in attractive dining room (beer only; guests may bring liquor), open to public 3 meals a day. Children welcome ($5 charge for crib or rollaway bed); pets at innkeeper's discretion (check in advance of stay). American Express, Diners Club, MasterCard and Visa credit cards accepted in dining room only. College tennis courts open to guests; community pool and golf course nearby. Excellent gift shop featuring crafts from college program. Campus tour twice daily.

DIRECTIONS: On I-75, 40 miles south of Lexington, take Berea exit 1 mile north to hotel.

Crafts are a specialty in this college town.

# BEAUMONT INN

Harrodsburg

## Where Southern belles met the *belles-lettres*

This is not Frontier Kentucky, this is Old South Kentucky. Once one walks through the fan-lighted front door there are numerous reminders that the sympathies here were solidly with the Confederacy. The entrance hall, for example, contains an admirable collection of pictures of Robert E. Lee.

The handsome Greek Revival brick building was for seventy years a school for southern young ladies. Annie Bell, a graduate who had become the school's president, and her husband, Glave Goddard, bought the buildings and opened the Beaumont Inn in 1919. It is still family-run: Chuck Dedman and his wife are fourth-generation innkeepers. Their fidelity to the family tradition is evident everywhere: in the lovely period-furnished living room, the guest rooms in the main building, and in the adjacent Beaumont Greystone and Beaumont Goddard Hall, and in the dining

room, once a college classroom. Classic southern cooking is well prepared and abundantly served.

The inn is an excellent base for those interested in historic Kentucky. Old Fort Harrod, a full-scale reproduction of the two hundred-year-old bastion, is nearby and well worth a visit, as is the Kentucky Horse Farm on the road to Lexington.

BEAUMONT INN, 638 Beaumont Drive, Harrodsburg, KY 40330; (606) 734-3381; Chuck Dedman and family, Innkeepers. An ante-bellum woman's college converted into a 29-room inn. Open all year. Rates $32 to $43, double occupancy; $9 for each extra adult in room. All rooms have color TV and private baths. Dining room, serving southern specialities, serves breakfast to guests, open to public for lunch and dinner; beer only, guests may bring liquor. Children welcome, extra charge $2.50 to $3.50 depending on age; no facilities for pets. MasterCard and Visa credit cards accepted. Lighted swimming pool, tennis courts and shuffleboard. Public golf course nearby. Gift shop.

DIRECTIONS: US 68, 30 miles south of Lexington, ¾ mile from downtown Harrodsburg south on US 127.

The sign says it all.

Harrodsburg # SHAKER VILLAGE **KENTUCKY**

## The beauty of simplicity

The Shakers are a curious part of America's religious heritage. A secessionist offshoot of the Quakers, their official name was "The United Society of Believers in Christ's Second Appearing." They believed in a dual God, an eternal father and mother, the parents of angels and men. At their religious services, both men and women would spontaneously launch into violently contortive dances, hence the nickname Shaking Quakers, or Shakers. They lived in communes, celibate, as brothers and sisters. And in their deliberate retreat from worldliness they produced some of the most exquisitely beautiful architecture, furniture and crafts that this country has ever seen.

Shaker Village at Pleasant Hill was founded in 1805, flourished for fifty years, then went into a slow decline, a victim, some say, of the Industrial Revolution. The village was officially closed in 1910; the last Quaker here died in 1923. At the zenith, more than five hundred Shakers worked Pleasant Hill's fifty-five hundred acres. They had a fine reputation for hospitality; every traveler who chanced by received a square meal and a night's lodging. After the bloody Civil War battle at nearby Perryville, the Shakers ministered to the wounded of both sides.

Shaker Village has been carefully restored in the past two decades at a cost of some eight million

dollars. Twenty-seven original buildings now are open to visitors. Guest are housed in the "family houses" and meetinghouse, two-story structures that retain the separate entrances for men and women. The rooms are faithful to the Shaker tradition, therefore simple in the extreme, but extraordinarily comfortable and consumately charming. Meals are prepared from traditional Shaker recipes and served at the handsome Trustee's House, where the elected leaders of the village conducted the necessary business with the outside world.

Shaker Village will reward the visitor who takes the time to explore it at leisure. The setting is beautiful, high on a hill above the river down which the Shakers barged their produce and goods to market in New Orleans. There are a number of craft demonstrations, and that rare wonder of wonders, a gift shop filled with unique and attractive merchandise.

*Left.* The inn buildings are all furnished with original pieces made by Shaker craftsmen. OVERLEAF. Quilts in traditional Shaker patterns are still being made by Armaphor Perkins, the last expert. The last page shows the steamboat "Dixie Belle" docked to take on passengers from the village.

SHAKER VILLAGE OF PLEASANT HILL INN, Rte. 4, Harrodsburg, KY 40330; (606) 734-5411; Ann Voris, Innkeeper. A historic site of 27 restored 19th-century Shaker buildings run by a non-profit educational corporation. Original family houses offer 70 rooms, all with private baths. Rates $36 to $64, double occupancy. Open all year. Dining room, featuring Shaker dishes, open to public for 3 meals a day (no wine or liquor; guests may bring own for use in accommodations only). Dining room closed Christmas Eve and Christmas Day. Children welcome (no charge for children under 18 years in room with parents); pets at discretion of innkeeper. No credit cards accepted; personal checks accepted with proper identification. Tour of grounds included in rates. A 150-passenger paddle wheel riverboat gives day cruises. Exceptional gift shop featuring Shaker furniture and crafts made on premises.

DIRECTIONS: Approximately 25 miles south of Lexington on US 68. Take by-pass New Circle Road 4. Exit west on Harrodsburg Pike to village.